BIG WEENIES

Written By:
Herbert Kavet

Illustrated By:
Martín Riskin

© 1993
by **Ivory Tower Publishing Company, Inc.**
All Rights Reserved

No portion of this book may be reproduced - mechanically, electronically, or by any other means including photocopying - without the permission of the publisher.

Manufactured in the United States of America

30 29 28 27 26 25 24 23 22 21 20 19 18 17 16 15 14 13 12 11 10 9 8 7 6 5 4 3 2 1

Ivory Tower Publishing Co., Inc.
125 Walnut St., P.O. Box 9132, Watertown, MA 02272-9132
Telephone #: (617) 923-1111   Fax #: (617) 923-8839

WHY DO SOME PEOPLE HAVE BIG WEENIES WHILE OTHER PEOPLE HAVE TEENIE WEENIES?

The reason some people have big weenies while other people have teeny weenies has to do with genetics. People who have teeny weenies wear their jeans too tight.

Every time they have a naughty thought (like imagining the deep, husky groaning of impatient, oiled coeds begging to be sated) or an erotic experience (like being crushed in the elevator against the soft, succulent, yielding body of Miss Weidemeyer from the typing pool) their weenies are prevented from achieving lift-off by the cruel, taut cords of their clinging clothes.

WHY DO SOME PEOPLE HAVE BIG WEENIES WHILE OTHER PEOPLE HAVE TEENIE WEENIES?

Not only that, but jeans are made of a material so dense that no light or air can get through, depriving the already-frustrated weenie of desperately needed light, air and its basic daily requirement of vitamin C, (as in Oh My God Did You See That!). Eventually, the little beggar just gives up, withers and dies.

So if you want to have a big weenie, you should dress in baggy pants and take it out a lot in public.

THE BIG WEENIE TEST

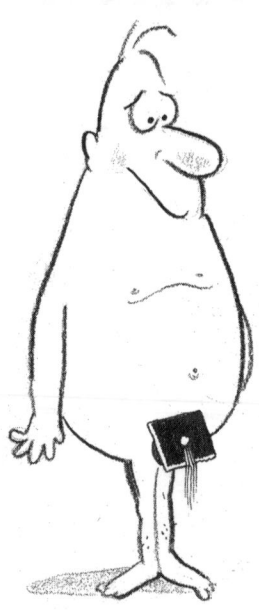

Men lie.
They will tell you they have a big weenie when all they have is a regular old, run-of-the-mill, average-size weenie. Or worse, a teeny weenie. All men should be made to take the official big weenie test.

THE PRICK

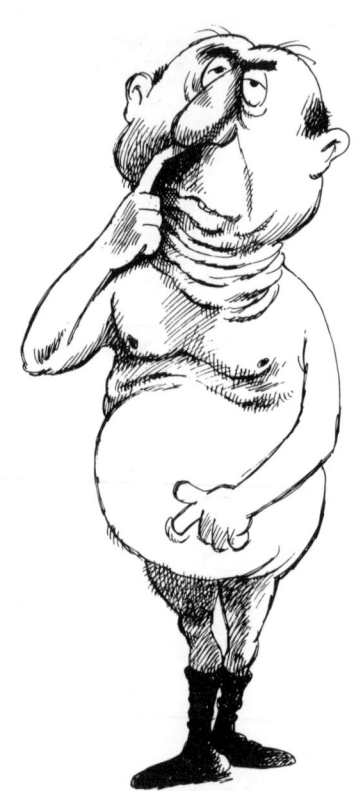

A particularly offensive type of male exists whose organ and, in fact, whose entire body is known as a PRICK. The PRICK male delights in rudeness and crass behavior. In kindergarten, he will crumble graham crackers onto the resting blankets of his classmates. In the primary school grades, he will purposely "lose" the pass to the bathroom causing untold hardship and misery to the other pupils. As he approaches puberty, itching powder in the kitty litter, eating mashed potatoes with his hands, making a collection of his own dandruff and arranging it in size order and forcefully helping old ladies BACK across the streets they have just crossed, are common practices.

Adulthood brings no change. Any man you see imitating the walk of fat ladies right behind them, sending back his martini more than once, razzing the strikeout of a Little Leaguer or driving with his finger in his nose will be a PRICK. The automobile owned by a PRICK will not start unless his finger is in his nose.

THE WEENIE

WEENIES are owned by two specific groups: accountants and efficiency experts. These men will tend toward small, clipped moustaches and groups of pens in their shirt pockets. Although neat dressers at work, at home they will usually wear old, torn bathrobes, Turkish slippers and, if alone, an occasional feather boa.

The WEENIE male will eat egg salad sandwiches for lunch five days a week. On the weekend, he will switch to peanut butter for excitement. He combines his sport with his hobby which is spearing the marshmallows in his cocoa with a toothpick and arranging them on black velvet into various patterns.

Men with WEENIES were the inventors and main propagators of the missionary position.

THE PHALLUS

This group is rather large. It includes all college professors, deans of any kind, flutists, all members of string quartets and anyone who majored in Philosophy or English Literature while at college.

Phallus owners tend toward beards and pipes with rainguards. They will have impeccable diction but find it impossible to carry a tune. They will invariably drive a Volvo with a ski rack although they will never actually ski, and they enjoy Mozart when it is played properly.

THE WEE WEE

The WEE WEE man will tend to be an elementary school teacher below the third grade, a librarian, or the owner of a sleep-away camp. He will be addicted to mittens, ear muffs and scarves except during the summer months and his hobby will be pony back riding. WEE WEE men are immature to a fault. They will be given to sudden petty fits of temper and will lock themselves in bathrooms. They will lean toward Teddy Bears in moments of stress and rarely finish all their vegetables.

WHERE DO BIG WEENIES GO...
WHEN THEY GET TEENY?

Ancient Vikings believed that when big weenies got teeny, they went to a great hall where beautiful handmaidens rubbed them with lox and scented water and smothered them with gentle affection until it was time to rise for battle again. Which explains why the weenies of ancient Vikings all smelled like a smothered lox.

Today, however, it is possible for us to be more medically accurate when addressing this important question. Today, we are reasonably certain that when big weenies get teeny, because, for example, they get rubbed the wrong way, they go to a place a lot like Philadelphia, because Philadelphia rubs everyone the wrong way.

THINGS YOU CAN DO WITH A BIG WEENIE THAT YOU CAN'T DO WITH A TEENY WEENIE

TEENY WEENIE

1. Make love to one cheerleader, leaving her unfulfilled.

2. Get your girlfriend's first initial tattooed on it.

3. If someone's trying to measure something, say, "If it helps, four of these make a foot."

BIG WEENIE

1. Make love to an entire cheerleading squad at once, leaving them unconscious.

2. Get the fully illustrated history of western civilization tattooed on it.

3. If someone's trying to measure something, say, "If it helps, you should set those wall studs about this far apart."

THINGS YOU CAN DO WITH A BIG WEENIE THAT YOU CAN'T DO WITH A TEENY WEENIE

TEENY WEENIE

4. Amuse your friends by putting sticky tape on the end of it and fishing a quarter from the bottom of a sugar bowl.

5. Get drunk and entertain a Dutchman by showing him a "new way to plug a small leak in his dyke."

6. Use it as a bookmark when you're reading in bed so you won't have to turn down the corner of the page and make the librarian angry.

BIG WEENIE

4. Amuse your friends by putting sticky tape on the end of it and fishing a Buick from the bottom of the East River.

5. Get drunk and entertain a Dutch dyke by plugging yourself while you're taking a leak.

6. Use it to make the librarian so you won't have to waste your time in bed reading.

THINGS YOU CAN DO WITH A BIG WEENIE THAT YOU CAN'T DO WITH A TEENY WEENIE

TEENY WEENIE

7. Get a cheap laugh at a party by saying, "Hey, I have a better way to press the remote channel changer."

8. Play a great practical joke at a wedding reception by putting a little mustard on it and slipping it onto a plate of cocktail weiners.

9. Cause your date to ask the question, "Is it in yet?"

BIG WEENIE

7. Get a cheap woman at a party by saying, "Don't bother getting up to change the channel. I can do it from here without using a remote."

8. Play a great practical joke at a wedding reception by painting it to look like a clarinet and asking the bride to "play a long, slow number so the rest of us can dance."

9. Cause your date to ask the question, "Is it all in yet!?"

THE MEMBER

All judges, attorneys, high school principals and insurance vice-presidents will have MEMBERS. They will use their MEMBER on a definite schedule, never on impulse, and only in total darkness, utilizing standard positions.

MEMBER bearers never remove their vests during sex and will use their extensive vocabularies while telling their bed partners:

a) what they did wrong

b) what they expect to happen next time

c) the possible consequences if it does not.

A disbarred attorney cannot have a MEMBER, although he will continue to call it that.

THE PICKLE

Any male involved in sales, particularly new cars, furniture or kitchen appliances, will sport a PICKLE. He will wear various sized checks at the same time, including his socks and tie, and spend much of his time participating in practical jokes involving noises. The PICKLE owner will begin talking in a loud voice at the age of three and will be totally bald by the age of thirteen. He will always breathe in your face while telling a joke. His only sport is blowing up whoopee cushions.

Some purchasing agents will imitate the brash demeanor of the PICKLE male in the hope of entering this category, but they only succeed in making spectacles of themselves.

THE PETER

Men who do physically hard labor have PETERS. Construction workers, lumberjacks, truck drivers and utility linemen are PETER people. The PETER personality is open and friendly. The PETER is treated like one of the boys and is often discussed as to size, usage and conditioning. The PETER potential of a PETER personality is usually not affected by alcohol. Research indicates that it is the frequency of arm wrestling while at the bar that keeps his sex drive at such a low level.

Men with PETERS still don't believe women should have orgasms.

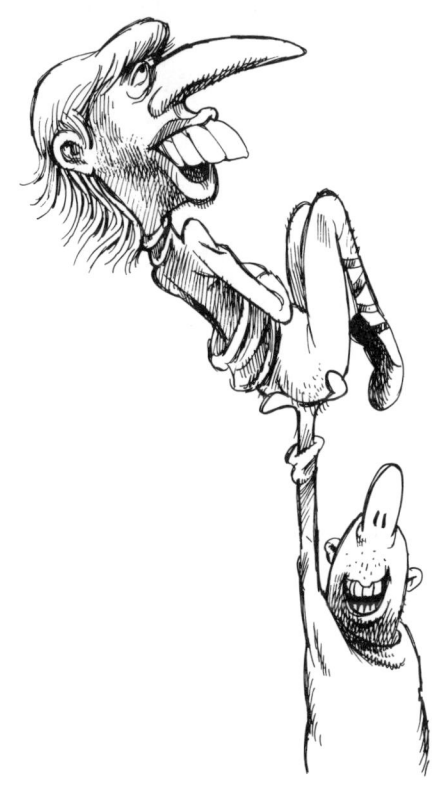

THE PRIVATE PARTS

Men who refer to their sexual organ as their PRIVATE PARTS are invariably involved in the arts. Authors, ballet dancers and choreographers are included here. Poets will embellish this into "Those PARTS most PRIVATE", while journalists often mention "My PRIVATE PARTS as they relate to the Third World." Males on the fringe of the art world such as agents, publishers and stage technicians refer to it as their SEMI-PRIVATE PARTS.

The PRIVATE PARTS person is given to long hair, leotards at home and a far-away look. He is never seen without a long scarf which he uses for washing and drying dishes, dusting, flair, a handkerchief and protecting his PRIVATE PARTS from the sun at nude beaches.

WHAT WOMEN LIKE ABOUT TEENY WEENIES

1. You can give teeny weenies cute names, like Mr. This-Won't-Hurt-A-Bit. That gets teeny weenies in the mood.

2. Teeny weenies come when you call them.

3. Afterwards, there's a little part of you still not satisfied, and you're left looking forward to the next time.

WHAT WOMEN LIKE ABOUT BIG WEENIES

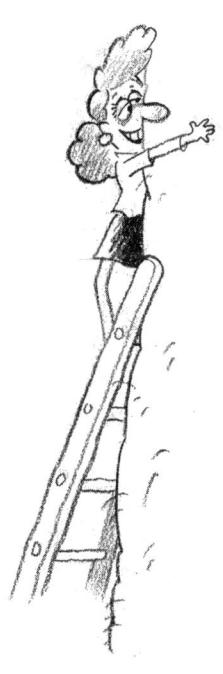

1. Who can remember some stupid cute name when you're crazy with lust? Grunting and pointing is all it takes to get big weenies in the mood.

2. Big weenies come and come and come when you call them.

3. Afterwards, there are little parts of you all around the room, and you're so satisfied you don't care if there's ever a next time.

WHEN YOU THINK YOU'VE FOUND A BIG WEENIE
and a Teeny Weenie pops up

Life is full of little surprises.

How do you handle the disappointment when one pops up?

What do you do when you've got a nine-story fire, and the fireman only has a one-story hose?

Experts say you have three alternatives.

WHEN YOU THINK YOU'VE FOUND A BIG WEENIE
and a Teeny Weenie pops up

THE THREE ALTERNATIVES
When you need a big weenie and a teeny weenie pops up, you can always:

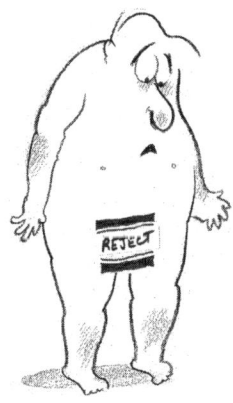

1. Duct-tape a whole bunch of teeny weenies together until you get a weenie big enough to make you happy.

2. Take it to Mr. Goodwrench, have him plug it into an air hose, and tell him not to take it out until you can read "GOODYEAR" on the side.

3. Hollow out a loaf of French bread, stuff it inside, and say, "Here's your chance to be a hero."

THE SCHLONG

It is well known that the SCHLONG is a sexual organ that is often double the size of the common male organ. Our research has discovered, however, the startling fact that one professional group, dentists, have ninety-eight percent of all the SCHLONGS found in North America. All dentists have SCHLONGS. Why this phenomenon has occurred is still unclear. Early indications are that leaning over people while drilling affects organ length and width in some manner.

The SCHLONG male, or dentist, if you will, is inordinately proud of his sexual organ. He will tend to display it on public transportation, will purposely dip while dancing and will show slides featuring himself at social functions in his home.

It is interesting to note here that not one SCHLONG owner has been found among all the orthodontists and oral surgeons examined by our staff.

THE COB

Many farmers call their organ a COB. COB men utilize those baggy overalls to hide an organ somewhat larger in size than most. They trust in suspenders, button-up flies and Republican administrations.

Unfortunately, many COB men do not know "which end is up" which, given their size, makes them dangerous lovers for petite women.

THE NO NO

There is a small group of men who have never stopped calling their sexual organ a NO NO. These men are always employed either by banks or the Internal Revenue Service. They are usually in their forties or fifties and are still living at home. The NO NO male never participates in sports, but has a multitude of hobbies. Among the more popular are saving string, stamp collecting and crocheting warming jackets for their NO NO's. The NO NO owner has a morbid fear of dust, insects, people with sniffles, women's NO NO's and germs. Any male seen backing away from a woman or wiping silverware at a restaurant is a NO NO male.

The NO NO owner always finishes his vegetables before having dessert.

THE DONG

The DONG is found only on doctors, mainly gynecologists and pediatricians. That unusual curve to the left has been attributed to a consistently faulty golf swing that throws the entire body, particularly the DONG, out of line with the spine. Anyone seen entering a restaurant sideways or always walking in diagonal lines is a DONG man. The DONG male's main interests in life are his golf game, walking toward his golf ball without veering and being able to putt without injury. He can be identified by his perpetual tan and the hundreds of small alligators sewn onto every article of his clothing.

It was a DONG man who discovered the "G" spot while searching for a lost golf ball.

How to Find a BIG WEENIE

Here's a clue:
Weenies grow in moist, dark places

To find a big weenie, you have to think like a big weenie. (Clue: Big weenies are always thinking, "I could sure go for a <u>dip</u> in a <u>damp</u>, <u>dark</u> place right about now.")

You have to act like a big weenie. (Clue: People are always telling big weenies, "Don't act so <u>stiff</u>. Relax, have a good time.")

You have to look like a big weenie. (Clue: Big weenies look a little up-<u>tight</u>, like they know they're going to have trouble fitting in.)

"Ergo, if you want to find a big weenie, you should slip on a pair of tights and get stiff with some dip in a cave."

WARNING

Sometimes A Big Weenie Looks Like A Teeny Weenie When It's Asleep

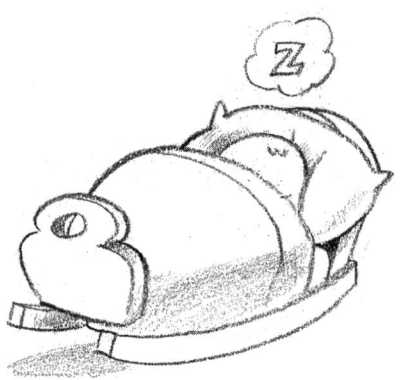

Too many people dismiss teeny weenies out of hand, forgetting the old expression, "Big things come in little packages."

Sometimes a teeny weenie will surprise you and turn out to be a big weenie that's taking a nap.

Sometimes you have to be patient. A big weenie is worth waiting for. Remember, it may be hard to admit to yourself later that you had a big weenie in your grasp and you blew it.

HOW TO FIND BIG WEENIES IN A STRANGE TOWN

How many times has this happened to you?

You're in a strange town, and you get a sudden, overwhelming urge for a big weenie. You feel yourself losing control, yet you don't know whom to ask for help, and you aren't even sure where to start looking.

What should you do? Run to a phone book and look up Weenies 'R Us?

I wish it were that easy.

Personally, I recommend the 4 Proven Techniques developed after much field testing and carefully monitored experimentation by the Russian national women's weight lifting team.

4 Proven Techniques For Finding Big Weenies in a Strange Town

1. Run to a phone book and look up Weenies 'R Us

2. Get a part-time job as a towel attendant at the Institute for the Exceptionally Well Endowed.

3. Take out a personal ad that begins, "Big Heated Space To Let."

4. Corner the night shift in an alley behind the local steel mill, tell them to drop their drawers for a surprise inspection, and just to show that you mean business, clean and jerk the plant foreman.

THE PUTZ

The professional range of the PUTZ male covers a broad spectrum. He can be found in all walks of life. Although difficult to classify by career or manner of employment, the PUTZEE is easily recognizable by noting the following behavioral traits.

All men have a PUTZ who tend to do two or more of the following:

1. Never give signals while driving
2. Tell the punch line of your joke with you
3. Take all the best hors d'oeuvres
4. Blow cigar smoke rings on your nose
5. Sit on your desk and drip doughnut jelly onto your reports.
6. Borrow your comb and pick their teeth with it

THE PRONG

Because the PRONG is unique among male sexual organs, the PRONG male is a man with problems. The almost constant erectile state of the PRONG can interfere with the work habits and social life of any male bearer. Although the PRONG is usually found on ladies' shoe salesmen, brassiere cutters and porno film managers, they have also been noted on jockeys, policemen and firemen above the rank of lieutenant, and, surprisingly, electrical engineers.

Beginning at puberty and continuing through the octogenarian years, the slightest stimulation can arouse the PRONG male into a state of readiness and, often, embarrassment. These arousal factors can range anywhere from the proximity of a female, to the grinding of automobile gears or ascending swiftly in an elevator. Due to fear of injury, the PRONG male never indulges in sports.

Multiple orgasms were invented by the wife of a PRONG man.

THE THING-A-MA-BOB

THING-A-MA-BOB's can be found on older government workers who work in small offices, writers of children's books, college presidents and all mathematicians. The THING-A-MA-BOB male will never be found without his hair neatly parted in the middle, a bow tie and socks held up over his knees by garters. He has had sex approximately 3.2 times in his life but does not recall with whom or why. He is extremely absent-minded and will give bones to his tropical fish and fish food to his dog. He will tend to forget where he works or where his THING-A-MA-BOB is located.

Men with THING-A-MA-BOB's always cover public toilet seats with paper.

THE SCHMECKEL

This little known name has been found to be exceedingly common to men in the television and movie world. Producers, directors and, in particular, actors, will classify their sexual organ with this name because of its tendency to enter the erectile state dozens of times each day. Interestingly, it is not usually the sight of an attractive female that is the cause of this. It is, rather, the sight of the owner himself, in mirrors or in glass store fronts that causes this frequent state of excitation.

It is not only his reflection that will tend to arouse the SCHMECKEL bearer. The sight of his ascot, his moustache wax, his baby pictures, the scent of his cologne or bath oil will cause the instant reaction described above.

The SCHMECKEL itself is of average length, but rather skinny.

MAKING A TEENY WEENIE GROW INTO A BIG WEENIE

Many people have been stuck with a teeny weenie.

They wonder, "What can I do to turn this teeny weenie into a big weenie?"

What about singing to it?

You'd be amazed at the change which you can bring about with a simple, throaty, sensuous song, a slow, pounding, passionate rhythm, and the steamy, smouldering, suggestive swaying of a wild-eyed, lust-crazed singer, hungry to taste the exquisite, forbidden, uninhibited joy of deep, penetrating and total fulfillment.

What can I tell you, it works for the spider plant.

MAKING A TEENY WEENIE GROW INTO A BIG WEENIE

What to Sing, What to Never Sing

If you want to make a teeny weenie grow into a big weenie, there are certain songs you should sing, and there are certain songs you should never sing.

You should sing tender songs, songs that nurture and build confidence (i.e. "You Are My Sunshine," or "Grow, Little Flower, Grow.") You should never sing songs that threaten or suggest violence (i.e. "Uh Oh, Uh, Oh, Here Comes The Sausage Grinder," or "Dance of the Scissors.")

The Weenie Songbook
- By The Light Of The Silvery Weenie
- Sentimental Weenie
- I Left My Weenie In San Francisco
- Chatanooga Weenie
- Standing On The Corner Watching All The Weenies Go By

You Should Sing:

"This Could Be The Start of Something Big"

"Great Balls of Fire"

"If I Had A Hammer"

"Put Your Head On My Shoulder"

"Tie Me Kangaroo Down"

You Should Never Sing:

"It Was An Itsy Bitsy, Teeny Weenie"

"Little Things Mean A Lot"

"It's A Small World After All"

"Short People"

"You Ain't Nothing But A Hound Dog"

MAKING A TEENY WEENIE GROW INTO A BIG WEENIE

Exercising Your Weenie

Another way to turn a teeny weenie into a big weenie is through rigorous exercise.

You should begin every day with the Royal Canadian Air Force Weenie Workout, a demanding, strenuous routine that includes:

20 Pumping Jacks	20 Squat Thrusts
20 Push-Ins	20 Sets of Humping in Place
20 Minutes of Intense Stretching	

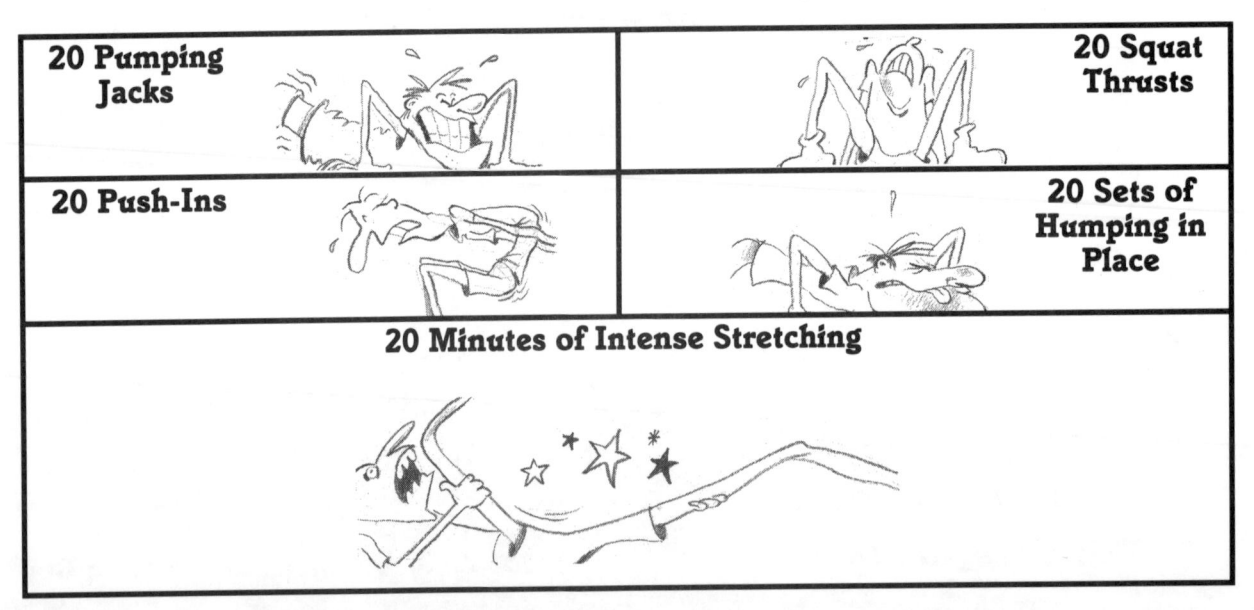

MAKING A TEENY WEENIE GROW INTO A BIG WEENIE

Exercising Your Weenie

If, on the other hand, you are a lazy, spineless yuppie who can't be bothered and is only interested in instant results, you can try the Royal Canadian Air Force Instant Weenie Workout: Tie your teeny weenie to a 3000-pound Clydesdale, then grit your teeth and show the horse a picture of Ed McMahon French-kissing Trigger.

MAKING A TEENY WEENIE GROW INTO A BIG WEENIE

TAKING YOUR WEENIE OUT FOR A GOOD TIME

Many weenies are teeny because they don't get taken out enough. This lack of exposure stifles their personal growth. If you don't want to be walking around with a stifled weenie, you should join the many people who have begun to take their weenies out all over town.

"Sounds great," you say, "but where should I go when I want to take my weenie out?"

Well, you should take it out someplace where it will fit in and feel comfortable.

I can recommend 5 places

MAKING A TEENY WEENIE GROW INTO A BIG WEENIE

TAKING YOUR WEENIE OUT FOR A GOOD TIME

When you feel like taking your weenie out, you can always:

1. Go to any take-out place. You'll be more than welcome, especially if you give them a little tip.

2. Better yet, go to any 24-hour take-out place. You'd be surprised at how many people get an urge to take out their weenie in the middle of the night.

3. Go to any sporting event. Weenies love to be in box seats. They also love it when you take them out to do the wave.

4. Take your weenie out to see Oprah. Maybe she'll put you on television. Talk about national exposure!

5. A health club is another great place to take your weenie out. I recommend going into the weight room and yelling out at the top of your lungs, "Hey, pump this!"

5 places to go when you want to take your weenie out

MAKING A TEENY WEENIE GROW INTO A BIG WEENIE

Nothing Beats A Good Massage In The End.

When it comes to turning a teeny weenie into a big weenie, nothing beats a good massage in the end.

Except having a plastic surgeon graft your weenie onto a hockey stick. Which is great until nine guys named Pierre grab it during face-off and try to use it to knock out each other's teeth.

SHOULD YOU PUT IT ON A LEASH?

There are three questions people with big weenies should ask themselves when trying to decide whether to put it on a leash:

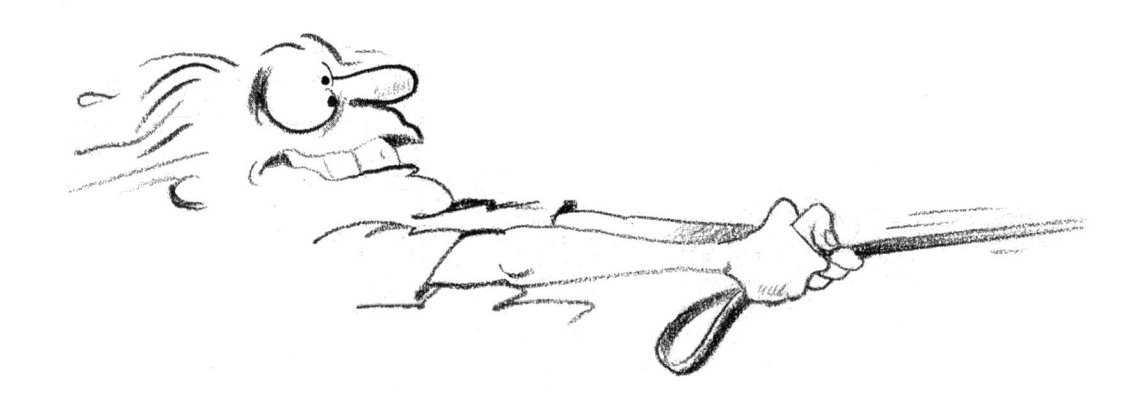

1. What are the chances it's going to get loose and run around turning over trash cans and making a general nuisance of itself?
2. What are the chances it's going to get loose and bite the postman?
3. What are the chances it's going to get an angry call from one of your neighbors saying to come on over, your weenie's made a mess on my porch?

THE JOINT

There is a small group of professional men, mainly lawyers and product managers, who, for reasons still to be determined, refer to their sexual organ as a JOINT. Perhaps because of the intense concentration required during their working hours, the rest of their day is spent squandering money on arcade games. Some have even been known to insert their JOINT into the coin slot when they run out of quarters.

JOINT men fantasize about group sex but the closest they get is going to see an X-rated movie with their friends.

THE WICK

It has been conclusively established that 96.7 percent of all professional athletes who are involved in any type of contact sport: hockey, boxing, basketball, football, soccer etc. are the bearers, however reluctantly, of a WICK. These sub-standard sized sexual organs are the direct result of years of confinement and abuse within jocks, cups and other types of protective paraphernalia. Although normally proportioned during his youth, the athlete's organ will grow progressively smaller throughout his playing years, the equipment and constant contact causing it to recoil protectively to a fraction of what should be its normal size.

The tiny proportions of the WICK wreak obvious havoc on the sex life of these athletes. This accounts for their hoarse yells and numerous temperamental displays while engaged in their individual sports. Fortunately, this situation is usually alleviated upon their retirement.
It was a WICK owner who discovered oral sex in 1948.

THE SEXUAL ORGAN

There is a specific group of men, high school and college biology and science teachers to be precise, who will refer to their sexual organ as their SEXUAL ORGAN. They will invariably be dressed in corduroy, speak in matter-of-fact tones about their SEXUAL ORGAN and point to it often while doing so. They love discussing their SEXUAL ORGANS. Their favorite sport is pointing vigorously to their own and other people's SEXUAL ORGANS, talking about them in a loud voice.

SEXUAL ORGAN owners don't urinate: they take leaks along public roads only partially concealed by bushes.

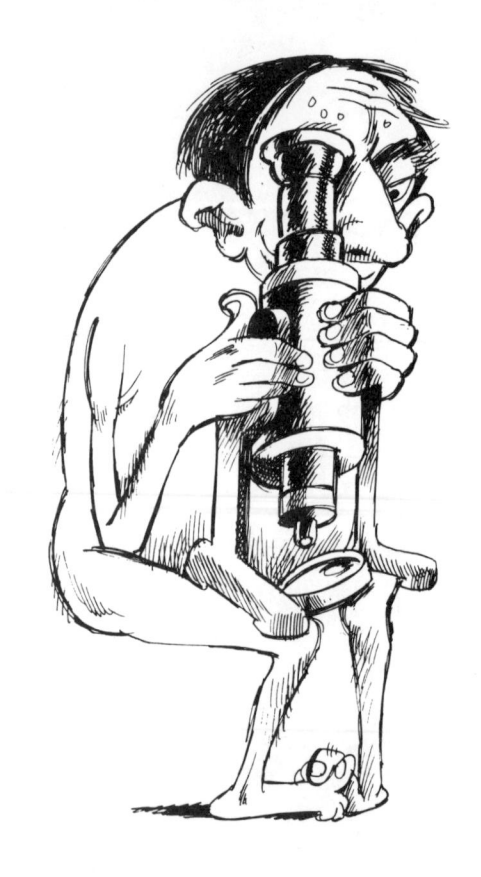

THE TOOL

Any man who drives a car made in Japan and who jogs more than 5 miles a week will have a TOOL. TOOLS tend to be thicker and larger than average and are forever getting caught in zippers. Men with TOOLS still call women "girls" or feel more comfortable with this term , and while they flirt outrageously, they are terrified of venereal diseases.

TOOL men think of themselves as great lovers but tend towards premature ejaculation.

BIG WEENIE EMERGENCIES

OOOOOH!
it's caught in my zipper

One of the occupational hazards of having a big weenie is that you keep getting it caught in your zipper. The great scientist, academic thinker and co-ed defoliator Albert "Two-Yard" Henderson, expressed it mathematically:

BW(big weenies) x **TP**(tight pants) ÷ **SZ**(steel zipper) + **UAH**(unexpected arrival of husband) = **3DWOT**(3 days of walking on your tiptoes)

What can you do when you get your weenie caught in your zipper?

Experts say you have 3 choices

WHEN YOUR WEENIE GETS CAUGHT IN YOUR ZIPPER

When your weenie gets caught in your zipper, you have 3 choices. You can:

1. Scream like a neutered tomcat, grab your throbbing weenie with both hands, and hop wildly around the room, smashing furniture, overturning chairs, and breaking whatever happens to be in your way until the pain goes away and all the other people in the restaurant stop gawking.

2. Scream like a neutered tomcat, grab your throbbing weenie with both hands, and hop wildly around the room, smashing furniture, overturning chairs, and breaking whatever happens to be in your way until the pain stops and all the other people in the restaurant agree to kiss it and make it better.

3. Cross your eyes, count to six thousand, and put it into something ice cold—like my wife.

WEENIE EMERGENCIES

What could be worse than getting your weenie stuck in your zipper?
Getting your weenie stuck in someone else's zipper.

At least <u>you</u> aren't going to jump up suddenly and decide to go out for a pizza.

What can you do when this happens to you? Experts say you have 3 choices.

WHEN YOUR WEENIE GETS STUCK IN SOMEONE ELSE'S ZIPPER

When your weenie gets stuck in someone else's zipper, you have 3 choices. You can:

1. Offer this other person many, many dollars not to move or breathe or let their body jerk convulsively with unchecked desire until you have had a chance to call the fire department and beg for the jaws of life.

2. Ignore the pain until you have satisfied all of your personal needs, then hope you pass out immediately afterwards.

3. Get down on your hands and knees and thank God it was not your tongue.

WEENIE EMERGENCIES

Wait A Minute, Wait A Minute, It's Probably Just Asleep

Some big weenies are sound sleepers. They will curl up and get all snugly and just lie there with their little mouth open, unconscious.

This can be very inconvenient, especially when you are naked with the all-Iowa women's bowling team at the time.

Here are 3 ideas:

What To Say When Your Weenie Won't Wake Up

When you can't seem to wake your weenie, there are only 3 things you can say:

1. "This happens from time to time. It has nothing to do with you personally. I hope you'll understand." (P.S. They won't understand.)

2. "This has never happened before. It must be you. This is not my fault." (P.S. There's about a 50-50 chance that saying this will get you shot.)

3. "This is a hundred dollar bill. It's yours if you promise never to breathe a word of this to another living soul." (P.S. There's about a 50-50 chance that word will be all over town by morning and that you'll never have another date as long as you live.)

THE SWORD

Monarchists, military officers and authoritative individuals who feel endowed with royal prerogatives call their organ a SWORD. SWORD owners try not to have sex with females who are beneath them in social stature, unless they have very large breasts or are willing to engage in acting out the SWORD owner's favorite fantasy. (This includes a crown, a full suit of armor and three ducks.)

SWORD males are easily recognized by the following behavioral characteristics:

1. They will have a look of easy confidence.
2. They will never turn their backs to any potential troublemaker.
3. They will casually unzip their flies at the first sign of trouble.

SWORD owners always send flowers after having intercourse.

THE SALAMI

This group is relatively small but very noisy. Many men who call their organ a SALAMI come from Brooklyn. They enjoy beer and, on the rare occasion when they wear a tie, invariably have mustard stains on it.

Women are "broads" and "chicks" to these boisterous fellows who never tire of elaborating on the one time they "made it" in the back seat of a car in Flatbush.

Men with SALAMIS wash <u>after</u> lovemaking and they never fail to stop at a mirror to comb their hair.

THE DOO HICKEY

All retired males are the possessors of DOO HICKEYs. The longer they are retired, the greater amount of items are referred to as DOO HICKEYs, so that eventually it becomes difficult to determine whether they are requesting sex or are talking about fiddling with some unknown gadget on their cars. A majority of DOO HICKEY owners purchase DOO HICKEY insurance as they tend to injure themselves while raking, zipping or closing shower doors.

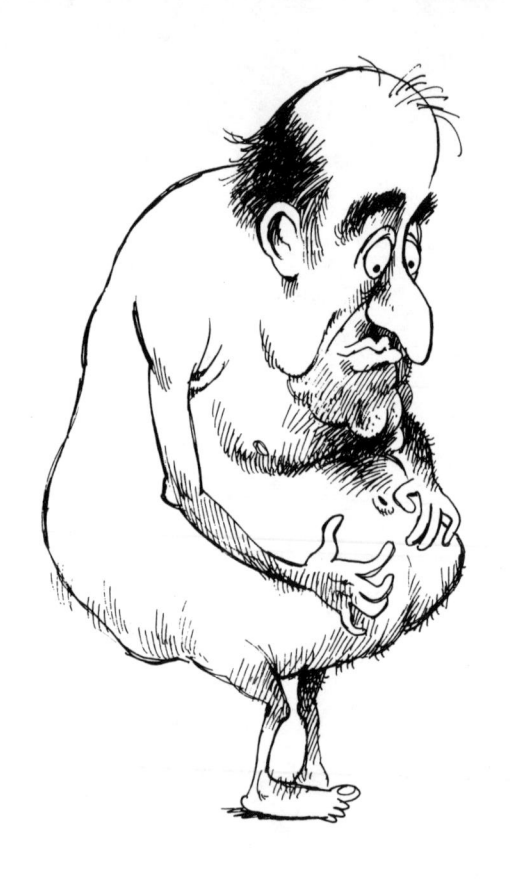

THE UNIT

UNIT owners include psychiatrists, psychologists, therapists of any kind and a majority of social workers. This label is a pseudonym, a cover up for their deep feelings of insecurity about the size and potential of their UNIT. This is sometimes known as the False Penis Syndrome. This group of males has good reason for their insecurity. There are clear indications that the nature of their work, sitting and listening cross-legged for hours on end, has an adverse effect on the size and function of their sexual organs. Their habit of wearing jockey shorts only adds to their problems. UNIT owners do not participate in sports because of embarrassment while undressing in locker rooms.

WHERE DO BIG WEENIES COME FROM?

What Women Think

Women think big weenies are a lot like the Loch Ness Monster: Exciting to think about but impossible to find.

They think when a man says, "I have a big weenie", he either:

1. Never learned the difference between 8-inches and 2-inches, or
2. Really means, "It's at home in a drawer along with my rubber Lassie blow-up doll, my Zorro suit, and my autographed copy of '365 Ways To Leave A Woman Unsatisfied'."

Women Have A Lot To Learn.

WHERE DO BIG WEENIES COME FROM?
What Men Think

When men think of big weenies, they think of the big bang theory.

They think, "Enough big bangs, and one day I'll get a big weenie."

Men are fools. They should know that you get a big weenie from slaloming on your tongue down the all-Nordic junior women's ski team.

THE DORK

Because of the limited intellectual capacity of the DORK male, his name has recently become synonymous with stupidity in common American usage. Besides watching lots of TV, there are numerous specific behavioral characteristics that make the DORK male readily identifiable.

The DORK male will often:

1. Light his cigarette in the middle

2. Make whiskey out of cotton instead of corn and then sleep it off in the clothes dryer

3. Believe politicians who promise to cut taxes

The DORK doesn't know his "ass from his elbow", which makes him very unpopular in gay bars.

THE ROD

The ROD male is found only in California. The entire male population of Burbank was found to have, or as they put it, pack RODS. A single male was found to have a ROD in Tulsa, Oklahoma, but further research uncovered a paternal grandfather from the Los Angeles area. The influence of Hollywood is clearly seen here, with the discovery of various curt offshoots, such as: LANCE, SPEAR, STICK, RIP, KICK, DENT, and in San Francisco, the BUFFY.

The ROD male is addicted to carrot juice, surfing and any type of sex that does not disturb his hair. When removed from his native coastal habitat, he'll continue to coat his ROD with #15 sunscreen.

THE PECKER

All auto mechanics, with the exception of those who work on expensive imports, all policemen and firemen up to the rank of lieutenant have PECKERS. The PECKER person will be argumentative about sports statistics, female erogenous zones and about his PECKER. He will tend to wear boxer type shorts one size too large for him and fishing hats with earflaps all year long.

PECKER people dislike

1. Disco music
2. Fresh fruits
3. Cats
4. White-on-white shirts.

Their favorite sport is drinking boilermakers and then standing in the surf up to their PECKER and casting onto the beach.

No PECKER has ever been found over 6 inches long.

THE THINGY

It has been recently discovered that 98.5 percent of all corporation executives are the possessors of THINGYs. Although the executives themselves never refer to their organ in this manner, preferring something more grandiose, this label has been given to their exceedingly tiny sexual organ by their wives and sweethearts and has been found to be correct, even generous by careful, scientific research.

Although normally proportioned at birth, the organ of these executives appears to shrink in direct proportion to the number of years on the job and their rise through the corporate ranks. The probable cause of this occupational hazard may be complete lack of usage due to nightly paper work, Commuter's Coma and four nightly martinis.

Regardless of the facts, as far as the executive is concerned, his THINGY is **GIGANTIC**.

WEENIES & CONDOMS
Condom Tips

It's important to select condoms that fit both your weenie and your life-style.

A man with a big weenie needs a big condom, while a man with a teeny weenie needs a big condom with a banana stuffed in the end.

Condoms come in eight sizes: small, medium, large, extra-large, Get The Crisco, Oh My God, Ohhhh My God!!!, and "Somebody call Roy and tell him Trigger's loose again."

How can you tell which size is right for you?
There is a simple 3-step test you can take.

WEENIES & CONDOMS

A Simple 3-Step Condom Size Test

You know you've got the wrong condom when:

1. It looks like after you put it on, you'll have enough latex left over to shrink-wrap Pittsburgh.

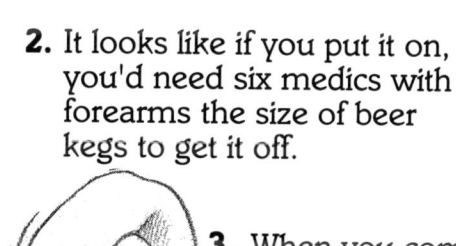

2. It looks like if you put it on, you'd need six medics with forearms the size of beer kegs to get it off.

3. When you come, it echoes.

THE PETZLES

Men who called their organs PETZLES mostly used to wheel pushcarts in old-fashioned ethnic neighborhoods. This has changed in recent years. Nowadays, men rarely refer to their organs by this name. More often it is a secretary or wife that will be heard referring to "his little PETZLE" or "not the PETZLE again."

Men who sport PETZLES usually go into their father-in-law's business and they always eat what's put before them, even string beans.

THE ROOT

ROOT males are one of the largest groups to be found in America today. They come from all walks of life but have two things in common: they live in the suburbs, and have an inordinate passion for gardening. All suburban males seen mowing, weeding, planting or transplanting are ROOT males.

The ROOT male loves to spend every moment of his leisure time "puttering" in his back yard. Because years of commuting have made him too tired for the physical act of sex, he has learned to sublimate, and achieves his erotic satisfactions by fondling the "roots" of plants and shrubs instead. The multiple benefits of this obvious sexual transference are threefold: prolonged titillation, sexual release without fatigue and higher real estate values.

THE PP

I know it sound silly, but many fully grown men still refer to their organ as a PP. While this childhood label persists among these men, it does not necessarily mean their PP is diminutive in size. One PP owner in Provincetown proudly sports a PP over 12 inches in length.

PP owners do exhibit the following traits:

1. They insist on window seats on airplanes and love to visit the pilot's compartment.

2. They drink Tang, believing the ads claiming astronauts used it.

3. Once toilet trained, PP males hardly ever remember to lift toilet seats.

Some PP males have been known to expose themselves at "Show and Tell" and they never remember the difference between foreplay and freeplay.

THE DICK

DICK bearers are found throughout the fifty states. All males who are joggers, racquetball players or tennis enthusiasts have DICKS. Additionally, anyone who shoots golf below one hundred is a DICK male.

DICK owners always have nice tans and will wear white articles of clothing only with little animals sewn on them. They love jocks, sprays of all sorts and their sneakers. They will often sleep with their white socks next to them on their pillows.

Although DICK males can be found on tracks, courts and golf courses, their natural habitat is the locker room. Most of the day is spent discussing their time, forehand or swing. During their leisure hours they will talcum each other and snap towels. Most DICK males never go home, preferring to sleep upright in their closed lockers suspended in their sweat pants from a hook.

WHO HAS BIG WEENIES?
WHO HAS TEENY WEENIES?

They have Big Weenies

Any man who has ever made a deposit at a sperm bank.

Any man named Steve.

Any man who needs to wear a jockstrap when he plays golf, to keep from accidentally knocking the ball off the tee.

They have Teeny Weenies

Any man who has ever made a withdrawal from a sperm bank.

Any man named Grace.

Any man who won't take a shower in the clubhouse after playing golf, to keep someone from mistaking it for a tee and trying to put it in his pocket.

WHO HAS BIG WEENIES?
WHO HAS TEENY WEENIES?

They have Big Weenies

Any man who is required by the FAA to strap a landing light to it so it won't endanger aircraft flying at night.

Any man who gets into an accident, then needs a separate stretcher for his weenie before they can carry him to the ambulance.

Any man who can't have sex unless he brings a can of Crisco.

They have Teeny Weenies

Any man who needs to tie a flare to it so he can find it at night.

Any man who gets into an accident, then is told by the ambulance driver, "Gee, I've never seen one of those things bitten off before."

Any man who can't have sex unless he brings a vibrator shaped like a can of Crisco.

THE SCHMUCK

The SCHMUCK can be found in any of the five New York boroughs. All taxi drivers are SCHMUCK males. They are a close-knit group and can be easily recognized by their habit of banding together in heavy traffic and calling to each other while waving one or more fingers out the driver's window. They never appear in public without their small caps, vests and cigar butts, which are specially made that size for them. Their favorite sports are honking their horns in accompaniment to their car radios and squeezing small rubber balls to strengthen their fingers.

SCHMUCK males regard any women who find them unattractive as "Frigid".

THE SHAFT

SHAFT males are found in every major metropolitan area in the United States. Although he cannot be classified by occupation, he is easily recognized by habitat, appearance and behavior. He can be found in singles bars, night clubs and discos between the hours of eleven P.M. and four A.M. His head and neck will be thrust forward due to the fact that he will be wearing fifteen to twenty gold chains. His shirt will be open to just above the groin area and his shoes will have metal taps in front and heel. His left hand will tap anything or anyone he is near, while the fingers of his right hand will snap to an inner beat. This tapping and snapping will continue unceasingly throughout the night.

The vocabulary of the SHAFT male is readily identifiable. He never has intercourse. He scores. He does not understand. He digs. Females are not women. They are birds, chicks, or dogs and in the Chicago area, strangely enough, armadillos.

The SHAFT male will disappear just before dawn. No one has ever seen a SHAFT male in direct sunlight.

THE PENIS

This label is used in medical circles only. No PENIS bearer will ever publicly refer to his organ in this manner because of the embarrassment involved. Doctors have only become aware of the PENIS during the past decade.

Males that call their penis a PENIS almost always have trouble maintaining an erection. This problem is psychosomatic in origin, almost always stemming from a traumatic experience during the male's first attempt at intercourse.

Some of the traumas that cause this problem include a female partner who:

1. Turned on the television set with her toe and then kept changing channels
2. Lighted a cigarette because she thought it was over
3. Asked him if it was Thursday
4. Told him she was going to be very busy during the next few months

THE SCHWANZ

Men who call their penis a SCHWANZ almost always have blond hair or wish they did. They take pride in their bodies, often working out with various complicated body building equipment each day. SCHWANZ men love to be touched and use their elbows and pelvic area to great advantage in crowded areas.

SCHWANZ men are good lovers and insist on making love with the lights on, but then they close their eyes. Many of these individuals have mastered the difficult task of faking orgasms.

PULLING A BIG WEENIE BONER AT THE BEACH

Embarrassing things can happen to you if you have a big weenie.

For example, you're walking along the beach and you pause in front of a beautiful woman, turning to profile your weenie as it strains dangerously against the sheer, supple fabric of your skin-tight, steel-belted swim briefs. Your eyes lock, your souls melt, and, moistening her lips, she raises herself to one elbow and says in an urgent, sultry voice, "Could you move it, Mac? Your weenie's blocking my sun."

What can you do? What can you say?

You have five choices

Snappy Comebacks When They Make Fun of Your Weenie on the Beach

Here are five things you can do or say:

1. Say, "Oops, you missed a spot on one of your chins."

2. Say, "You aren't the one who wanted to go for a ride on the war canoe?"

3. Say nothing. Walk into the water, lie on your back, run a sail up your mast, and wait to be blown to another continent.

4. Say nothing. Walk into the water, lie on your back, run a sail up your mast, and wait to be blown.

5. Turn quickly to leave, using your weenie to coldcock the bitch.

PULLING A BIG WEENIE BONER IN A CROWDED ELEVATOR

Did this ever happen to you?

You're in a crowded elevator when Mister Happy makes an unexpected visit. Before you know it, the six people in front of you are demanding that you lower your umbrella. Then they notice you don't have an umbrella.

What can you say?

TRY:

"Hey, is it my fault you remind me of sheep?"

"I always get on the elevator when I want to get off. Want to get off with me?"

"Who farted?"

PULLING A BIG WEENIE BONER ON THE DANCE FLOOR

You're at the office Christmas party minding your own business when the big boss's secretary pulls you out onto the floor for a slow dance. The lights are low, the room is crowded, and you've had 12 Scotches. Putting your arm carefully and respectfully around her back, you discover that she's not wearing a bra, and without warning, your weenie swells to the size of a lifeboat. What should you say?

You can always try:

1. "So, how do you think the Packers will do this year?"
2. "I hope I'm not chafing your leg."
3. "Please stand up. Everybody's looking."

THE DOBBER

Men who are balding refer to their organ as a DOBBER. Many DOBBER owners work as stockbrokers, insurance "consultants", tax shelter advisors and other kinds of semi-respectable occupations involving separating people from their hard earned money.

In their quest for relief from their daily mathematical grind, DOBBER men often turn to the more imaginative forms of sex. Leather, rubber, sex aides and kinky underwear of all kinds are bought by these seemingly well-dressed fellows.

Once this book is published, DOBBER men will probably start calling their penises something else.

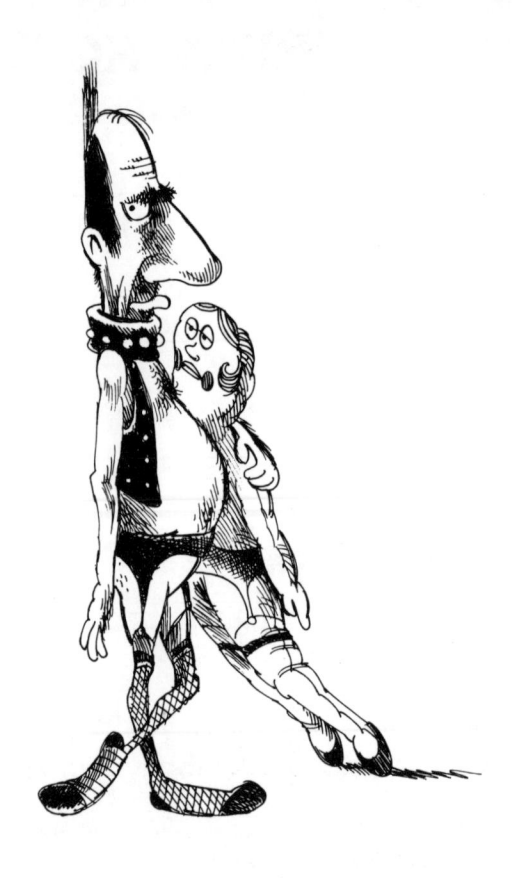

THE WANG

All males who work with computers have WANGS. They are meticulous dressers, punctual to a fault and often wear bow ties. Although highly sexual, the WANG male rarely consummates. He simply finds fiddling with his computer more satisfying.

Even though WANG owners are excellent providers, few women are content to stay involved with them. The wives of WANG men have lovers who think "Software" refers to some new kind of comfortable underwear.

THE BANANA

Swarthy, hairy men who often speak with accents or in regional variations of English using words like "Youse Guys" or "Heyyyah" call their organs BANANAS. Many of these "guys" work in food businesses or drive trucks. These men often speak in a vocabulary that is unintelligible to outsiders. For example:

"The avocados of your zone are erogenous."
Translation: "The knees of your wife are outrageous."

"Banjo, Harold. Low down Nazi. Do my nuts deceive me? Are you losing your kamquarts?"
Translation: "Hello, Harold. Long time, no see. Do my eyes deceive me? Are you losing your hair?"

BANANA owners are almost totally ignorant of the existence of foreplay.

THE COCK

Men who call their organ a COCK are generally inordinately proud of their member. They thrill in their virility and prowess with women, and often examine their COCK in a mirror when it is in an erect state. As youths they tended toward excessive masturbation. Owners of COCKS are quite prevalent in upper middle management positions, but not quite as upper as they think. COCK males are mortified by their first inability to achieve an erection and often turn to alcohol for consolation.

IT TAKES TWO HANDS TO HANDLE A WHOPPER

If you've ever been to a fire and seen the firemen lose control of their hose, well, you know it's not a pretty sight.

Hey, no one wants to lose control of their hose. That's why, if you've got a big weenie, it's not a bad idea to invite a few of the women from the office to come by and give you a hand the next time you're planning to use it.

Your wife or girlfriend will be touched by your thoughtfulness. Trust me.

RATING YOUR BIG WEENIE
Let's See What You've Got

THE DOGLEG LEFT

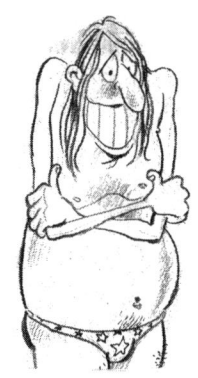

Also known as the "Liberal Love Spike" for its left-leaning tendencies, the Dogleg Left resembles a gold club in that it spends most of it's time banging into your balls. People with Dogleg Lefts like experimental sex, making love on tweed sheets, aftershave that smells like guilt, and getting tied up and spanked by K-Mart management trainees. Dogleg Lefts make great lovers as long as you don't get turned off by the saliva.

THE SPRINGBOARD

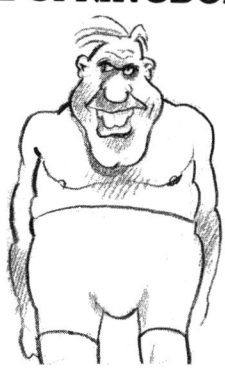

Springboards are weenies that combine many of the most desirable physical properties of Spandex, pig iron, and popcorn. Elastic, durable and great with butter, the good news is that they tend to stay taut and bouncy for days. The bad news is that if you want to go out later for pizza, you'd better wear a large barrel. Men with Springboards like to attend dinner parties and go diving with the hostess. Many perish in revolving door accidents.

RATING YOUR BIG WEENIE
Let's See What You've Got

THE DOGLEG RIGHT

The Dogleg Right is the weenie of preference for Republican women. Rigid and unbending, hard-nosed and inflexible, firm and unyielding, the Dogleg Right is common to men with conservative taste and bad hairpieces. In fact, many say the taste reminds them of toupee paste. Those with Dogleg Rights excel at racquet sports and spend a lot of time in the shower working on their backhand. They believe in good, clean, healthy sex as long as it doesn't cost more than $20. No Dogleg Right has ever gotten lucky with twins.

THE THOROUGHBRED

Thoroughbreds are big, beautiful weenies that are known for speed rather than endurance. They like to be ridden hard and respond well to the whip. If you're dressed in silk and wearing spurs, so much the better. Graceful, powerful, high-strung and intense, Thoroughbreds must be kept under tight rein at all times or they tend to explode out of the box, or worse, fall behind and finish in the rear. The next time you want to find a Thoroughbred, try looking under any woman with a British accent.

RATING YOUR BIG WEENIE
Let's See What You've Got

THE WALKING STICK

These slender, polished, hard-as-hickory weenies are equally as handy for beating off crowds of admirers in the park as they are for just beating off in the park. Many find the doorknob-sized head of Walking Stick weenies useful for coldcocking airline stewardesses. Forty-three percent of all men with Walking Sticks have had a mistress. But they wore her out before the other fifty-seven percent could get a crack at her. All Walking Sticks are mouth-breathers and are especially attractive to people with butt tucks.

THE DYNAMITE STICK

If you have a Dynamite Stick, then you have a weenie that can go off at any time. Unpredictable and extremely volatile, this weenie gives new meaning to the expression, "explosive sex". This is not to say that Dynamite Sticks have a problem with premature ejaculation; typically, none have been able to hold out that long. No Dynamite Stick has ever had a second date.

RATING YOUR BIG WEENIE
Let's See What You've Got

THE FIREPLUG

Short, stout, and real popular with dogs, what this weenie lacks in length is more than made up for by its grotesque width. Pound for pound, being pounded by a Fireplug is about as much fun as being porked by a Studebaker. No one with a Fireplug has ever completely satisfied a collie.

THE BATTERING RAM

The Cadillac of big weenies, the Battering Ram is the most formidable weapon in love's tender arsenal. Sleek enough to rate a chorus of Ohhhhhhs, generous enough to set off an avalanche of Ahhhhhhs, this weenie is also powerful enough to overcome even the stiffest resistance to its urgent advances. It is not uncommon for men with Battering Rams to walk down the street and have people behind them stop and whisper, "What a prick".

RATING YOUR BIG WEENIE
Let's See What You've Got

THE DEFLATOR

The Deflator is a kind of weenie that grows to the size of a mule's back leg during foreplay, only to shrivel up like a dead catfish when its time to get down to serious business. Nothing can revive a shrivelled Deflator, although scientists are experimenting with a cure that involves the use of a large suede suppository and a fungo bat. Men with Deflators are known for their 8-second intercourse, 3-date relationships, and 1-position mentalities.

THE RELUCTANT DRAGON

The Reluctant Dragon is the sleeping giant of the weenie world. Slow to anger, it remains dormant through the most persuasive attempts to arouse it from its natural, limpid state. Many people have developed debilitating hand cramps, lockjaw, and knee-burn from trying. Nonetheless, seeing a Reluctant Dragon rear its magnificent head in search of fresh prey can be a sight you'll carry to your grave, which is where many love partners wind up due to terminal frustration. Men with Reluctant Dragons are always late for parties and French-kiss like chickens.

THE DIPSTICK

Men who have an inordinate interest in the automobile almost inevitably are bearers of DIPSTICKS. While DIPSTICK organs appear normal when at rest, in the erectile state they will bend downward at the halfway point, sort of forming an inverted V.

The DIPSTICK male will tend to be shy with women and rarely attempts intercourse due to fear of rejection. When he does attempt it, it will only be with a woman who is anatomically correct for him and these, understandably, are extremely difficult to find. Besides, finding these women takes time away from their cars.

Although normal in surface appearance, the DIPSTICK male has been discovered to have specific behavioral patterns. Any male observed doing the following will be a DIPSTICK male.

1. Driving with only one hand

2. Wearing sunglasses on cloudy days

3. Insisting on premium unleaded gas

THE BONE

Among restauranteurs, chefs, diner owners and fast food restaurant managers, the sexual organ is commonly referred to as a BONE.

BONE owners always hire the best-looking young girls to work at their restaurants. They fantasize about "making it" with these women in the storage room, but can rarely induce them to enter it alone.

Men who call their organs a BONE love to touch themselves. They are the sole reason for the signs in restaurant toilets admonishing the help to wash their hands.

THE STINGER

Men who live by the sea or own boats of any kind usually have STINGERS. The STINGER males's entire body seems to be one large erogenous zone. Perhaps this comes about from the bracing salt air or the large amount of oysters consumed. Unfortunately, however, a STINGER male rarely mates. The fault lies in the extremely curved shape of this sexual organ. Although intercourse itself does not present a serious problem, it is the retrieval of his organ, aptly named STINGER, that causes the difficulty.

Because of its odd shape, the following physical symptoms occur to the STINGER male upon withdrawal.

1. His ears will flap forward violently
2. He will tend to swallow his tongue
3. His eyes will cross, sometimes irrevocably
4. His cheeks will pinch in and he will bite them
5. His Adam's apple will bob up and down furiously

It is easy to understand why men with STINGERS hate to "get involved".

THE MY MEAT

The large sexual organ of the MY MEAT male is generally carried by a body resembling a Neanderthal man. The dietary preferences and cultural inclinations of this individual are, to put it nicely, basic.

Most MY MEAT males take commercial courses in high school and the very few who go on to college take two phys. ed. courses before flunking out. Entering the business world, MY MEAT men go into trucking or sales and earn inordinate amounts of money.

MY MEAT males refuse to use KY jelly and are all divorced by the age of 30.

Other books we publish are available at many fine stores. If you can't find them, send directly to us. $7.00 postpaid

2400-How To Have Sex On Your Birthday. Finding a partner, special birthday sex positions, kinky sex on your birthday and much more.

2402-Confessions From The Bathroom. There are things in this book that happen to all of us that none of us ever talk about. The Gas Station Dump, for example, or the Corn Niblet Dump, the Porta Pottie Dump and more.

2403-The Good Bonking Guide. Bonking is a great new British term for doing "you know what". Covers bonking in the dark, bonking all night long, improving your bonking, and everything else you've ever wanted to know.

2407-40 Happens. When being out of prune juice ruins your whole day and you realize anyone with the energy to do it on a weeknight must be a sex maniac.

2408-30 Happens. When you take out a lifetime membership at your health club, and you still wonder when the baby fat will finally disappear.

2409-50 Happens. When you remember when "made in Japan" meant something that didn't work, and you can't remember what you went to the top of the stairs for.

2411-The Geriatric Sex Guide. It's not his mind that needs expanding; and you're in the mood now, but by the time you're naked, you won't be!

2412-Golf Shots. What excuses to use to play through first, ways to distract your opponent, and when and where a true golfer is willing to play.

2414-60 Happens. When your kids start to look middle-aged, when software is some kind of comfortable underwear, and when your hearing is perfect if everyone would just stop mumbling.

2416-The Absolutely Worst Fart Book. The First Date Fart, The Oh My God Don't Let Me Fart Now Fart, The Lovers' Fart, The Doctor's Exam Room Fart and many more.

2417-Women Over 30 Are Better Because... Their nightmares about exams are starting to fade and their handbags can sustain life for about a week with no outside support whatsoever.

2418-9 Months In The Sac. A humorous look at pregnancy through the eyes of the baby, such as: why do pregnant women have to go to the bathroom as soon as they get to the store, and why does baby start doing aerobics when it's time to sleep?

2419-Cucumbers Are Better Than Men Because... Cucumbers are always ready when you are and cucumbers will never hear "yes, yes" when you're saying "NO, NO."

2421-Honeymoon Guide. Every IMPORTANT thing to know about the honeymoon — from The Advantages Of Undressing With The Light On (it's slightly easier to undo a bra) to What Men Want Most (being allowed to sleep right afterwards without having to talk about love).

2422-Eat Yourself Healthy. Calories only add up if the food is consumed at a table. Snacking and stand up nibbling don't count. Green M&M's are full of the same vitamins found in broccoli and lots of other useful eating information your mother never told you.

2423-Is There Sex After 40? Your wife liked you better when the bulge above your waist used to be the bulge in your trousers. You think wife-swapping means getting someone else to cook for you.

2424-Is There Sex After 50? Going to bed early just means a chance to catch up on your reading or watch a little extra t.v., and you find that you actually miss trying to make love quietly so as not to wake the children.

2425-Women Over 40 Are Better Because... Over 90 reasons why women over 40 really are better: They realize that no matter how many sit-ups and leg raises they do, they cannot recapture their 17-year-old figures—but they can find something attractive in any 21-year-old guy.

2426-Women Over 50 Are Better Because... More reasons why women over 50 are better: They will be amused if you take them parking, and they know that being alone is better than being with someone they don't like.

2427-You Know You're Over The Hill When... You tend to repeat yourself. All the stories of your youth have already bored most acquaintances several times over. Even worse, you've resigned to being slightly overweight after trying every diet that has come along in the last 15 years.

2428-Beer Is Better Than Women Because (Part II)... A beer doesn't get upset if you call it by the wrong name; and after several beers, you can roll over and go to sleep without having to talk about love.

2429-Married To A Computer. You're married to a computer if you fondle it daily, you keep in touch when you're travelling and you stare at it a lot without understanding it. You even eat most meals with it. Truly advanced computers are indistinguishable from coke machines.

2430-Is There Sex After 30? By the time you're 30, parking isn't as much fun as it was in high school. He thinks foreplay means parading around nude in front of the mirror, holding his stomach in; and she has found that the quickest way to get rid of an unwanted date is to start talking about commitment.

2431-Happy Birthday You Old Fart! You're an Old Fart when you spend less and less time between visits to a toilet, your back goes out more than you do, you tend to refer to anyone under 40 as a "kid," and you leave programming the VCR to people under 25.

2432-Big Weenies. Why some people have big weenies while other people have teenie weenies; how to find big weenies in a strange town; rating a weenie; as well as the kinds of men who possess a putz, a prong, a schwanz, a member, a rod and a wang—and more!

2433-Games You Can Play With Your Pussy. Why everyone should have a pussy; how to give a pussy a bath (grease the sides of the tub so it won't be able to claw its way out); dealing with pussy hairs (shellac it so the hairs stay right where they belong); and everything else you ever wanted to know about pussies.

2434-Sex And Marriage. What wives want out of marriage (romance, respect and a Bloomingdale's Charge Card); what husbands want out of marriage (to be left alone when watching football games and to be allowed to go to sleep after sex).

Ivory Tower Publishing Co., Inc., 125 Walnut St., P.O. Box 9132, Watertown, MA 02272-9132   Tel: (617) 923-1111